The Children's Catechism

A Bible Verse Memory System
for Churches and Families

Second Edition

Scripture quotations are from the ESV® Bible (The Holy Bible, English Standard Version®), copyright 2001 by Crossway, a publishing ministry of Good News Publishers. Used by permission. All rights reserved.

By
Dr. Matthew Everhard

Acknowledgements

This children's catechism was originally designed for use in Faith Evangelical Presbyterian Church (EPC) in Brooksville, Florida. The first edition was edited by Sasha Barker. The second edition was edited by Emily Carpenter and Kristi Prada. The cover graphic is by Cathryn Sheldon Canfield. Faith Church would like to thank all of the above for their work on this project. Special thanks are given to Crossway Publishers for the use of the ESV in this Second Edition. Any remaining faults in this work are of course my own.

Matthew Everhard

"Train up a child in the way he should go; even when he is old he will not depart from it." (Proverbs 22:6)

Preface: A Letter to Parents

By the time your child graduates from high school, he or she will have watched more hours of television (15,000) than he or she will have spent in the educational classroom (12,000). If we were to compare children's hours of television consumed verses hours in Sunday School, the statistics are so dismal I can hardly bring myself to mention them! But I will. Assuming your child had 100% participation and rarely missed Sunday School, he or she would log just over 1,000 hours in Biblical instruction, a scant 1/15th of his or her time in front of the television. Add video games to the equation and my calculator breaks—not to mention my heart. To stem the gap, we (Christian believers) need to find more excellent ways to educate our children in the foundational truths of the Scriptures, especially at home! To do this, I propose that we "go back in time," to an age-old process known as "catechism" (from the Greek word meaning 'instruction').

I hope that the small booklet that you have in your hands will become a very important component of your child's discipleship. In this short work, I have endeavored to create a tool with which parents, Sunday School teachers, and Christian educators can educate their children in the ancient method of catechism.

For generations, believers have sought to educate their children through the tried and true method of rote memorization. While many adults today shrink back at the thought of disciplined memorization, we must not forget that children in elementary school have been blessed by God with the gift of brains like sponges!

The concept of catechesis can be traced back many, many generations. My inspiration for this little booklet came primarily through the great piece of literature called the "Westminster Shorter Catechism" written by the Puritans in England and Scotland in 1647. The goal of the Puritans was to help their families memorize and thoroughly master theology. In the

American colonies, the Westminster Shorter Catechism came into the homes of Christian believers in the form of the New England "Primer," a wonderful document by which children learned to read and write—right out of the Bible and the Westminster Standards!

The primary "advance" that I have put forth in this new work is that every single question is answered with a quotation of Scripture. Thus, when a child memorizes an answer, he or she has also acquired a piece of Scripture, right out of the Bible! I have taken care to ensure that all the answers, even the short ones, are faithful to the Holy Bible in their original context. All the while, children are integrating this information into a thoroughly Christian worldview.

My desire is that parents, teachers, pastors, and other believing adults would take the job of training the next generation seriously.

How to Use this Book

The goal for this booklet is that the information taught in the Sunday School classroom will be parallel to that which is taught in the home. My hope is that students from kindergarten through fifth grade will have memorized this catechism by the time they enter middle school.

First of all, you will notice that the catechism is broken down into sections by topical category. This will help parents and teachers work on sections that coincide with themes that may be ongoing in the Sunday School classroom curriculum.

Also, each section contains answers to questions that are short, as well as answers that are longer. Obviously, younger children will do well to focus on those questions with shorter, concise answers. At the same time, older children will be expected to move on to more advanced responses.

When a child memorizes a particular answer, he or she will have the delight of placing a sticker in their catechism booklet! Take it from my own children, Soriah, Elijah, and Simone - this can be great fun! Meanwhile, as parents utilize this catechism at home, Sunday School teachers may also monitor their progress with charts in the classroom. Again, stickers, prizes, and rewards ought to be given out liberally to keep the children motivated and encouraged.

Perhaps when a child memorizes the entire catechism, he or she will be brought to the front of his or her church to be recognized by the entire congregation! The more we celebrate our children's accomplishments, the more they will enjoy their own diligent work.

Enjoying God, after all, is the primary goal of our lives! As one Reformed catechism asked many years ago: *What is the chief end of man? Answer: Man's chief end is to glorify God and enjoy Him forever!*

Dr. Matthew Everhard
Pastor, Faith Evangelical Presbyterian Church
Brooksville, Florida

1

Creation and the Fall

"And God blessed them. And God said to them, "Be fruitful and multiply and fill the earth and subdue it." (Genesis 1:28)

1. Who made everything?
Answer: "In the beginning, God created the heavens and the earth." (Genesis 1:1)

2. What did God think about all He had made?
Answer: "God saw that it was good." (Genesis 1:25)

3. How did God make people?
Answer: "So God created man in His own image." (Genesis 1:27)

4. From what did God make Adam?
Answer: "Then the Lord God formed the man of dust from the ground." (Genesis 2:7)

5 From what did God make Eve?
Answer: "And the rib that the Lord God had taken from the man He made into a woman." (Genesis 2:22)

6 For what reason did God put Adam and Eve in the Garden of Eden?
Answer: "To work it and keep it." (Genesis 2:15)

7 What did God say to Adam that he must never do?
Answer: "But of the tree of the knowledge of good and evil you shall not eat, for in the day that you eat of it you shall surely die." (Genesis 2:17)

8. What did Adam and Eve do with the forbidden fruit?
Answer: Adam and Eve "took of its fruits and ate." (Genesis 3:6)

9. What consequence did Adam face after he ate from the tree?
Answer: "Therefore the Lord God sent him out from the Garden of Eden." (Genesis 3:23)

10. What else happened to Adam because of his sin?
Answer: "Because of Adam's sin, "he died." (Genesis 5:5)

11 Who else has sinned like Adam and Eve?
Answer: The Bible says, "For all have sinned and fall short of the glory of God." (Romans 3:23)

12 What do those who sin deserve?
Answer: "The wages of sin is death." (Romans 6:23)

2

The Commandments of God

"You shall love the Lord your God with all your heart and with all your soul and with all your mind." (Matthew 22:37)

1. What is the First Commandment?

Answer: The First Commandment is "You shall have no other gods before me." (Exodus 20:3)

2. What is the Second Commandment?

Answer: The Second Commandment is "You shall not make for yourself a carved image." (Exodus 20:4)

3. What is the Third Commandment?

Answer: The Third Commandment is "You shall not take the name of the Lord your God in vain." (Exodus 20:7)

4. What is the Fourth Commandment?

Answer: The Fourth Commandment is "Remember the Sabbath day, to keep it holy." (Exodus 20:8)

5. What is the Fifth Commandment?

Answer: The Fifth Commandment is "Honor your father and your mother." (Exodus 20:12)

6. What is the Sixth Commandment?

Answer: The Sixth Commandment is "You shall not murder." (Exodus 20:13)

7 What is the Seventh Commandment?
Answer: The Seventh Commandment is "You shall not commit adultery." (Exodus 20:14)

8 What is the Eighth Commandment?
Answer: The Eighth Commandment is "You shall not steal." (Exodus 20:15)

9 What is the Ninth Commandment?
Answer: The Ninth Commandment is "You shall not bear false witness against your neighbor." (Exodus 20:16)

10 What is the Tenth Commandment?
Answer: The Tenth Commandment is "You shall not covet." (Exodus 20:17)

11 What did Jesus say is the most important commandment given?
Answer: Jesus said the most important commandment is "You shall love the Lord your God with all your heart and with all your soul and with all your mind." (Matthew 22:37)

12. What did Jesus say is the second most important commandment?
Answer: Jesus said, "And a second is like it: You shall love your neighbor as yourself." (Matthew 22:39)

13. On the night Jesus was betrayed, He gave a new command; what is it?
Answer: Jesus said, "A new commandment I give to you, that you love one another." (John 13:34)

3

Theology:
The Nature of God

"I am God, and there is none like me." (Isaiah 46:9)

1 What is God?
Answer: "God is spirit, and those who worship him must worship in spirit and truth." (John 4:24)

2 Is God good or bad?
Answer: "For the Lord is good; his steadfast love endures forever." (Psalm 100:5)

3 God revealed His divine name to Moses; what is it?
Answer: God said to Moses, "I am who I am." (Exodus 3:14)

4. What name did Jesus call God that we can call Him as well?
Answer: Jesus called God "Father." (Matthew 6:9)

5. Is God loving?
Answer: The Bible says, "God is love." (1 John 4:16)

6. How many gods are there?
Answer: "God is one." (James 2:19)

7. Are there any other gods?
Answer: No! The Lord said, "For I am God, and there is no other." (Isaiah 45:22)

8. God exists in three Persons; what are their names?
Answer: "The name of the Father and of the Son and of the Holy Spirit."
(Matthew 28:19)

9. Since God is loving and holy, what should His people do?
Answer: We should "Serve the Lord with gladness!"
(Psalm 100:2)

10. What does God deserve due to His greatness?
Answer: God deserves "honor and glory forever and ever."
(1 Timothy 1:17)

Is God all-powerful?
Answer: Yes!
"For nothing will be impossible with God." (Luke 1:37)

 How does God demonstrate His love for us?
Answer: "God shows His love for us in that while we were still sinners, Christ died for us." (Romans 5:8)

4

Jesus: The Son of God

"This is my beloved Son, with whom I am well pleased."
(Matthew 3:17)

1. Why did God send His Son?

Answer: "For God so loved the world, that he gave his only Son, that whoever believes in him should not perish but have eternal life." (John 3:16)

2. Why did Jesus come into the world?

Answer: "Jesus came into the world to save sinners." (1 Timothy 1:15)

3. Did Jesus ever sin?

Answer: Jesus never sinned. "But one who in every respect has been tempted as we are, yet without sin." (Hebrews 4:15)

4. What did God the Father say about the Son?
Answer: God said of Jesus, "This is my beloved Son; listen to him." (Mark 9:7)

5. How is the Son like the Father?
Answer: "He is the radiance of the glory of God and the exact imprint of his nature." (Hebrews 1:3)

6. What did Jesus say that proves that He is one with the Father?
Answer: Jesus said, "I and the Father are one." (John 10:30)

7 What is the only way that Jesus said we can come to God?
Answer: Jesus said, "I am the way, and the truth, and the life. No one comes to the Father except through me." (John 14:6)

8 Is there any other way to be saved except through Jesus?
Answer: "There is no other name under heaven given among men by which we must be saved." (Acts 4:12)

9 How did Jesus save us?
Answer: Jesus saved us "by the blood of his cross." (Colossians 1:20)

10 What happened to Jesus after He died?

Answer: After Jesus died "he rose from the dead."
(Acts 10:41)

11 What happened to Jesus after He rose from the dead?

Answer: After Jesus rose "he was carried up into Heaven."
(Luke 24:51)

12 Where is Jesus right now?

Answer: Jesus is now "at the right hand of God."
(Acts 7:55)

5

The Holy Spirit

"When the Spirit of truth comes, he will guide you into all the truth." (John 16:13)

1. Who is the Third Person of the Trinity?
Answer: The Third Person of the Trinity is "the Holy Spirit." (Matthew 28:18)

2. Where did Jesus promise that the Holy Spirit will live?
Answer: The Holy Spirit "dwells with you and will be in you." (John 14:17)

3. What did Jesus promise that the Holy Spirit will do for us?
Answer: The Holy Spirit will "teach you all things and bring to your remembrance all that I have said to you." (John 14:26)

4. What does the Holy Spirit give us power to do?

Answer: The Bible says, "You will receive power when the Holy Spirit has come upon you, and you will be my witnesses." (Acts 1:8)

5. How has God's love been poured into our hearts?

Answer: "God's love has been poured into our hearts through the Holy Spirit who has been given to us." (Romans 5:5)

6. Who are the sons of God?

Answer: "All who are led by the Spirit of God are sons of God." (Romans 8:14)

7 How do we know that we are God's children?
Answer: "The Spirit himself bears witness with our spirit that we are children of God." (Romans 8:16)

8 When did the Early Church experience a great outpouring of the Spirit?
Answer: "The day of Pentecost." (Acts 2:1)

9 What did the Early Church do when they experienced His power on the day of Pentecost?
Answer: "They were all filled with the Holy Spirit and continued to speak the word of God with boldness."

(Acts 4:31)

10 Does the Holy Spirit help us to pray?
Answer: Yes. "Likewise the Spirit helps us in our weakness. For we do not know what to pray for as we ought." (Romans 8:26)

11 How can an unbeliever receive the Holy Spirit?
Answer: "Repent and be baptized every one of you in the name of Jesus Christ for the forgiveness of your sins, and you will receive the gift of the Holy Spirit." (Acts 2:38)

12. What is the Fruit of the Spirit?

Answer: "The fruit of the Spirit is love, joy, peace, patience, kindness, goodness, faithfulness, gentleness, and self-control." (Galatians 5:22-23)

6

Salvation

"And there is salvation in no one else, for there is no other name under heaven given among men by which we must be saved." (Acts 4:12)

1. What did God do in His great love for us?

Answer: "For God so loved the world, that he gave his only Son, that whoever believes in him should not perish but have eternal life." (John 3:16)

2. What must we do in order to go to heaven when we die?

Answer: The Bible says, "Believe in the Lord Jesus, and you will be saved." (Acts 16:31)

3. Doesn't everyone go to Heaven when they die?

Answer: No! Jesus said, "You must be born again." (John 3:7)

4. Are we saved by our good works or by our faith?

Answer: "For by grace you have been saved through faith. And this is not your own doing; it is the gift of God, not a result of works, so that no one may boast." (Ephesians 2:8-9)

5. What is faith?
Answer: "Now faith is the assurance of things hoped for, the conviction of things not seen." (Hebrews 11:1)

6. What should we do when we sin?
Answer: We should "Repent, for the Kingdom of Heaven is at hand." (Matthew 3:2)

7. What will happen when we confess our sins?
Answer: "If we confess our sins, he is faithful and just to forgive us our sins and to cleanse us from all unrighteousness." (1 John 1:9)

8. Did we choose God or did God first choose us?
Answer: Jesus said, "You did not choose me, but I chose you." (John 15:16)

9. When did God choose us?
Answer: God chose us "before the foundation of the world." (Ephesians 1:4)

10 On what basis did God choose us?

Answer: "In love he predestined us for adoption to himself as sons through Jesus Christ." (Ephesians 1:4-5)

11 Jesus said there is one sure way that others will know we are His disciples; what is it?

Answer: Jesus said, "By this all people will know that you are my disciples, if you have love for one another." (John 13:35)

12 Can a Christian ever fall away from grace?

Answer: A Christian cannot fall away, for Jesus said, "no one will snatch them out of my hand." (John 10:28)

7

The Sacraments of the Church

"Go therefore and make disciples of all nations, baptizing them in the name of the Father and of the Son and of the Holy Spirit."
(Matthew 28:19)

1 What holy meal, called a sacrament, does the Church eat together?
Answer: "The Lord's Supper."
(1 Corinthians 11:20)

2 When did Jesus institute the Lord's Supper?
Answer: Jesus instituted the Lord's Supper "on the night he was betrayed."
(1 Corinthians 11:23)

3 What did Jesus do with the bread on the night He was betrayed?
Answer: "When he had given thanks, he broke it, and said, "This is my body, which is for you. Do this in remembrance of me."
(1 Corinthians 11:24)

4 What did Jesus do with the cup after His last supper?
Answer: "He took the cup, after supper, saying, "This cup is the new covenant in my blood. Do this, as often as you drink it, in remembrance of me." (1 Corinthians 11:25)

5 Why do we celebrate the Lord's Supper?
Answer: We celebrate the Lord's Supper to "proclaim the Lord's death until he comes." (1 Corinthians 11:26)

6 In addition to the Lord's Supper, what is the other "sacrament?"
Answer: "Baptism." (Romans 6:4)

7 With what do we baptize?
Answer: "Water."
(1 Peter 3:21)

8 How many times must we be baptized?
Answer: "One."
(Ephesians 4:5)

9 What does baptism symbolize?
Answer: Baptism symbolizes "new life."
(Romans 6:4)

10 In whose name should we baptize?
Answer: We baptize "in the name of the Father and of the Son and of the Holy Spirit."
(Matthew 28:19)

11. What did Jesus say that we should teach those who are baptized?
Answer: Jesus said, teach them "to observe all that I have commanded you."
(Matthew 28:20)

12. Is the promise of baptism just for adults?
Answer: No, Peter said it is "for you and your children."
(Acts 2:39)

8

Spiritual Warfare

"For the weapons of our warfare are not of the flesh but have divine power to destroy strongholds."
(2 Corinthians 10:4)

1. Will Christians face many difficulties in this life?
Answer: Yes. "Through many tribulations we must enter the kingdom of God." (Acts 14:22)

2. What should we do when we suffer?
Answer: We should "rejoice in our sufferings, knowing that suffering produces endurance." (Romans 5:3)

3. Against whom must Christians struggle?
Answer: Christians struggle "against the spiritual forces of evil in the Heavenly places." (Ephesians 6:12)

4 Who is the chief enemy of our souls?

Answer: The enemy of our souls is "the devil." (1 Peter 5:8)

5 How does the devil attack?

Answer: Our "adversary the devil prowls around like a roaring lion, seeking someone to devour." (1 Peter 5:8)

6 What must we do when the devil attacks?

Answer: We must "Resist him, firm in your faith." (1 Peter 5:9)

7. What is the first piece of armor that God has given us to protect ourselves?
Answer: For our protection, God gave us "the belt of truth." (Ephesians 6:14)

8. What has He given us to protect our hearts?
Answer: To protect our hearts, God gave "the breastplate of righteousness."
(Ephesians 6:14)

9. What shall we put on our feet?
Answer: We must put on "the readiness given by the gospel of peace." (Ephesians 6:15)

10. What have we been given to stop the flaming arrows of the evil one?
Answer: To stop the arrows of the evil one, God gave "the shield of faith." (Ephesians 6:16)

11. What piece of armor is to be placed upon our heads?
Answer: "The helmet of salvation." (Ephesians 6:17)

12. What weapon should we carry in our hands?
Answer: We should carry "the sword of the Spirit, which is the Word of God." (Ephesians 6:17)

9

Prayer

"Evening and morning and at noon I utter my complaint and moan, and he hears my voice." (Psalm 55:17)

1. To whom should Christians pray?
Answer: "My prayer is to you, O Lord." (Psalm 69:13)

2. Jesus gave us a wonderful prayer called the Lord's Prayer. How did He tell us to begin the prayer?
Answer: We begin the prayer by saying, "Our Father in Heaven, hallowed be your name." (Matthew 6:9)

3. What is the second request in the Lord's Prayer?
Answer: May "your Kingdom come." (Matthew 6:10)

4 What is this third request in the Lord's Prayer?
Answer: May "your will be done on Earth as it is in Heaven." (Matthew 6:10)

5 What is the fourth request in the Lord's Prayer?
Answer: "Give us this day our daily bread." (Matthew 6:11)

6 What is the fifth request in the Lord's Prayer?
Answer: "Forgive us our debts, as we also have forgiven our debtors." (Matthew 6:12)

7. What is the sixth request in the Lord's Prayer?
Answer: "Lead us not into temptation, but deliver us from evil." (Matthew 6:13)

8. What else may we pray about?
Answer: We may pray about "everything." (Philippians 4:6)

9. On what occasions shall we pray?
Answer: We can pray "at all times in the Spirit, with all prayer and supplication." (Ephesians 6:18)

10. When shall we stop praying?

Answer: We must never stop praying for the Bible says, "pray without ceasing."
(1 Thessalonians 5:17)

11. Does prayer really work?

Answer: Yes! "The prayer of a righteous person has great power as it is working."
(James 5:16)

12. As a child of God, what can I be sure of?

Answer: I can be sure that "the Lord accepts my prayer."
(Psalm 6:9)

10

The Christian Family

"Fathers, do not provoke your children to anger, but bring them up in the discipline and instruction of the Lord."
(Ephesians 6:4)

1. How must Christians view marriage?
Answer: Christians believe: "Let marriage be held in honor among all." (Hebrews 13:4)

2. What happens when a man marries a woman?
Answer: A man and his wife marry and "become one flesh." (Genesis 2:24)

3. What should a Christian man and woman do when they love one another, and cannot resist being together?
Answer: "Let them marry." (1 Corinthians 7:36)

4. How long does a Christian marriage last?
Answer: A Christian marriage is for life. Paul says, "A wife is bound to her husband as long as he lives."
(1 Corinthians 7:39)

5. Who ought to lead by godly example in a Christian household?
Answer: "For the husband is the head of the wife even as Christ is the head of the church." (Ephesians 5:23)

6. If the husband is the head, what role is the wife?
Answer: She is "a helper fit for him." (Genesis 2:18)

7. In what way ought the husband love his wife?
Answer: A husband must love his wife "as Christ loved the church and gave himself up for her." (Ephesians 5:25)

8. What does the Bible say about a godly wife?
Answer: A godly wife "is far more precious than jewels." (Proverbs 31:10)

9. How must we regard godly women?
Answer: "A woman who fears the Lord is to be praised." (Proverbs 31:30)

10 What does the Bible teach wives to do in regard to their husbands?
Answer: It says, "Wives should submit in everything to their husbands." (Ephesians 5:24)

11 What must a godly man do to lead his family?
Answer: A godly man "must manage his own household well, with all dignity keeping his children submissive." (1 Timothy 3:4)

12 What does the Bible teach children to do in regard to their parents?
Answer: The Bible says, "Children, obey your parents in the Lord, for this is right." (Ephesians 6:1)

11

Heaven and Hell

"Then I saw a new heaven and a new earth, for the first heaven and the first earth had passed away."
(Revelation 21:1)

1. What does the Bible call the place that believers go to when they die?
Answer: "Heaven." (Revelation 21:1)

2. What is the greatest blessing for those in heaven?
Answer: The best part of heaven for believers is that "God himself will be with them." (Revelation 21:3)

3. To what is heaven compared?
Answer: "The Holy City, new Jerusalem." (Revelation 21:2)

4. Will anyone in Heaven be sad or in pain?
Answer: In heaven, "He will wipe away every tear from their eyes, and death shall be no more, neither shall there be mourning, nor crying, nor pain anymore." (Revelation 21:4)

5. Will Heaven need anything to give it light?
Answer: No! "And the city has no need of sun or moon to shine on it, for the glory of God gives it light." (Revelation 21:23)

6. Will there be any sin in heaven?

Answer: There will be no sin in heaven, for "Nothing unclean will ever enter it." (Revelation 21:27)

7. How long will the joys of Heaven last?

Answer: The joys of Heaven will endure "forever and ever." (Revelation 22:5)

8. What is this place of punishment called?

Answer: God's place of punishment is called "hell." (Matthew 5:22)

9 What will happen to those who do not believe in Jesus?
Answer: Those who do not believe "will suffer the punishment of eternal destruction, away from the presence of the Lord and from the glory of his might." (2 Thessalonians 1:9)

10 What is Hell like?
Answer: Hell is a place of "torment." (Luke 16:23)

11 To what is Hell compared?
Answer: Hell is like a "lake that burns with fire and sulfur." (Revelation 21:8)

12. What will happen in Hell to the devil and anyone who rejects God's love in Jesus Christ?

Answer: Those who reject God's love in Christ "will be tormented day and night for ever and ever."
(Revelation 20:10)

Made in the USA
Monee, IL
17 November 2021